$ 15.00

RIO VISTA SCHOOL
AB 862

04/05

THE MAGIC OF LANGUAGE

Adjectives

By Ann Heinrichs

THE CHILD'S WORLD®
CHANHASSEN, MINNESOTA

The Child's World

Published in the United States of America by The Child's World®
PO Box 326, Chanhassen, MN 55317-0326
800-599-READ
www.childsworld.com

Content Adviser:
Kathy Rzany, M.A.,
Adjunct Professor,
School of Education,
Dominican University,
River Forest, Illinois

Photo Credits: Cover photograph: Punchstock/BananaStock Interior photographs:
Animals Animals/Earth Scenes: 18 (John C. Stevenson), 22 (Robert Lubek), 25
(Werner Layer); Corbis: 11, 15 (Jose Luis Pelaez Inc.), 17 (Henry Diltz), 20 (Tony
Arruz); Getty Images/FoodPix/Susan C. Bourgoin: 28; Norbert Schaefer/Corbis: 8, 24;
PictureQuest: 5 (Geoff Butler/eStock Photo), 27 (Janis Christie/PhotoDisc).

The Child's World®: Mary Berendes, Publishing Director

Editorial Directions, Inc.: E. Russell Primm, Editorial Director; Pam Rosenberg,
Project Editor; Melissa McDaniel, Line Editor; Katie Marsico, Assistant Editor;
Matt Messbarger, Editorial Assistant; Susan Hindman, Copyeditor; Susan Ashley and
Sarah E. De Capua, Proofreaders; Chris Simms and Olivia Nellums, Fact Checkers;
Timothy Griffin/IndexServ, Indexer; Cian Loughlin O'Day and Dawn Friedman,
Photo Researchers; Linda S. Koutris, Photo Selector

The Design Lab: Kathleen Petelinsek, Design and Page Production;
Kari Thornborough, Page Production Assistant

Library of Congress Cataloging-in-Publication Data
Heinrichs, Ann.
  Adjectives / by Ann Heinrichs.
    p. cm. — (The magic of language)
Includes index.
Contents: What is an adjective?—Predicate adjectives—Big, bigger, and biggest—
Fewer kids? less fun!—Three little articles—Nouns that act like adjectives—Whose is
it?—Pronouns that act like adjectives—More pronouns that act like adjectives—Fun
with numbers and opposites.
  ISBN 1-59296-067-7 (library bound : alk. paper)
  1. English language—Adjective—Juvenile literature. [1. English language—Adjective.]
I. Title. II. Series: The Magic of Language.
  PE1241.H37 2004
  428.2—dc22   2003020037

TABLE OF CONTENTS

CHAPTER ONE

4 What Is an Adjective?

CHAPTER TWO

7 Predicate Adjectives

CHAPTER THREE

9 Big, Bigger, and Biggest

CHAPTER FOUR

13 Fewer Kids? Less Fun!

CHAPTER FIVE

15 Three Little Articles

CHAPTER SIX

19 Nouns That Act Like Adjectives

CHAPTER SEVEN

21 Whose Is It?

CHAPTER EIGHT

24 Pronouns That Act Like Adjectives

CHAPTER NINE

26 More Pronouns That Act Like Adjectives

CHAPTER TEN

28 Fun with Numbers and Opposites

30 How to Learn More

31 Fun with Adjectives

32 Index

32 Answers

CHAPTER ONE

WHAT IS AN ADJECTIVE?

Do you have a **noisy** dog on your block? Is your desk

squeaky? What is the **longest** book you've ever read?

What do you like to do on a **sunny** day?

All the blue words above are adjectives. You can use adjectives to

describe people and things, activities, and just about everything!

DEFINITION

An **adjective** is a word that modifies, or describes, a noun or pronoun.

Many adjectives answer the question "what kind?" They might

show color, size, or shape. They can tell what something is made of or

how it feels.

A red sailboat glides on blue water on a sunny afternoon. How many adjectives are in the previous sentence? If you counted three, you are correct!

EXAMPLE

A **round** peg won't fit in a **square** hole.

We sailed in a **red** boat.

My **fuzzy** mittens keep me **warm.**

Some adjectives end in *-y,* such as **squeaky, empty,** and

chilly. Some have special endings, such as *-able, -al, -ful, -ive,*

-less, and *-ous.* Examples are **lovable, logical, careful,**

attractive, careless, and **dangerous.** Other adjectives end with *-ed* or *-ing,* such as **wilted** and **blooming.**

Adjectives can make a story come alive! They can add interest, excitement, or surprise. It's fun to think of unusual adjectives to describe something. These examples show you can make more than one choice:

EXAMPLE

scary	spooky, creepy, hair-raising
loud	blaring, screeching, shrill
big	huge, enormous, gigantic

TRY THESE!

Think of more colorful adjectives for these words:

good   old   little   great   quiet

See page 32 for the answers. Don't peek!

CHAPTER TWO

PREDICATE ADJECTIVES

Where is the adjective? Its usual place is right before the word it describes. However, an adjective can also come after a linking verb.

An adjective in this position is called a predicate adjective. Like other adjectives, it describes a noun or pronoun. It answers the question "what is it like?"

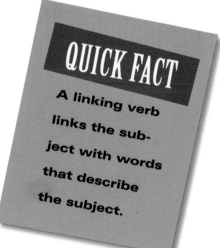

QUICK FACT

A linking verb links the subject with words that describe the subject.

EXAMPLE

BEFORE THE NOUN	PREDICATE ADJECTIVE
I have a **cozy** room.	My room is **cozy**.
These are **tiny** dogs.	These dogs are **tiny**.
We have a **talented** mouse.	Our mouse is **talented**.
That was an **exciting** movie.	That movie was **exciting**.
These are **dull** scissors.	These scissors are **dull**.

As you see, each predicate adjective describes the subject of the sentence. The linking verbs are forms of the verb "to be." Other link-

ing verbs work the same way:

EXAMPLE

> Mr. Yee seems **tired.**
>
> This milk tastes **funny.**
>
> The twins act **silly.**

*These twin sisters are identical. Can you find the predicate adjective in the last sentence? If you guessed the word **identical**, then you are right!*

CHAPTER THREE

BIG, BIGGER, AND BIGGEST

EXAMPLE

Erin is **tall,** and Aaron is **taller,** but Alexis is **the tallest** of all.

This example shows how you can use adjectives

to compare things.

DEFINITION

The **comparative form** of an adjective compares two things.

If you have two **big** dogs, one is probably **bigger.** If two **fast** cars zoom by, one is probably **faster.** If you ate two **delicious** desserts yesterday, one was probably **more delicious!**

Some adjectives build the comparative form by adding -er, as in

shorter and **softer.** Others use "more" or "less," as in **more important** and **less famous.**

Comparatives often use **than** when comparing two things.

EXAMPLE

This banana is bigger than that carrot.
My pillow is harder than the floor!
Is math more interesting than spelling?
Skating is less dangerous than skateboarding.

Of all your pencils, one is **the sharpest.** Think about your socks. Which pair is **the most colorful?** Do you like scary stories? Which one is **the scariest of all?**

As you see, **the** usually comes before a superlative adjective. Some superlatives are formed by adding -est. Maybe you've met **the**

DEFINITION

The **superlative form** of an adjective compares three or more things.

*This little kitty might win a fluffiest kitty cat contest. In that case, the word **fluffiest** is the superlative adjective because we are saying there are none more fluffy than this cat.*

fluffiest kitty or **the funniest** clown. Other superlatives use

"most" or "least." You might have **the most difficult** exam or

the least comfortable shoes.

A few adjectives have irregular comparative and superlative

forms. They don't add *-er* or *-est,* and they don't use more, most, less, or least. Some examples are **good–better–best** and

bad–worse–worst.

TRY THESE!

Name the comparative and superlative forms of these adjectives:

dark young new strong expensive

See page 32 for the answers. Don't peek!

Some adjectives cannot be compared to anything else. You cannot use "more" or "the most" with them. Suppose you found the **per-fect** outfit to wear. No outfit could be more perfect or the most perfect. That's because nothing is better than **perfect!**

WATCH OUT!

Never use a double comparison. One is enough! You would never say "more bigger" or "most longest."

12

CHAPTER FOUR

FEWER KIDS? LESS FUN!

There are lots of other ways to compare things. But watch out!

Some of them are very tricky!

What if two things are *not* different? Can you still compare them?

Yes! Just use **as . . . as.**

EXAMPLE

Julian is as smart as Ally.

You can use **as . . . as** to compare things that are different,

too. Just include **not.**

EXAMPLE

My cat is not as scary as your dog.

Now get ready to strain your brain! We're going to compare quan-

tities. We'll use the adjectives **more, less, much, little,**

fewer, many, and **few.**

Let's start with **fun** and **air.** You cannot count fun or air. Fun is just *there,* and so is air. But you still might want to compare how much is there. For things you can't count, use the adjectives **more, less, much,** and **little.**

EXAMPLE

Spiderman is *more* fun than the Hulk.
Superman is *less* fun than Wonder Woman.
My balloon has *less* air than yours.
My rabbit is *as much* fun as a monkey.
This tire has *as little* air as a pancake.

Now let's take **kids** and **balloons.** You can count kids, and you can count balloons. For things you can count, use the adjectives **more, fewer, many,** and **few.**

EXAMPLE

Our team has *more* kids than the other team.
This class has *fewer* kids than the one next door.
We have *fewer* balloons than they do.
We invited as *many* kids as we could.
We found as *few* balloons as our teacher did.

CHAPTER FIVE

THREE LITTLE ARTICLES

There are three little words that you use all the time, but you hardly think about them. Can you guess what they are? They are **a, an,** and **the.** These three words are called articles.

Articles are adjectives. They don't really describe anything. Instead,

*She is a girl. In this last sentence, **a** is the article. We need articles before nouns because it would sound silly to say "she is girl."*

they are used to introduce a noun. Without the article, something

seems to be missing! Just look:

EXAMPLE

WITHOUT AN ARTICLE
Here comes elephant.
Give me apple.
I'd love to ride camel.

WITH AN ARTICLE
Here comes **the** elephant.
Give me **an** apple.
I'd love to ride **a** camel.

The is called a definite article. It's

used to introduce a specific noun. Maybe

that noun has been mentioned before.

Maybe the **the** refers to only one possi-

ble noun. Maybe the reader or listener

already knows what is being discussed.

DID YOU KNOW?
Grammar rules are slightly different in England than in the United States. For example, when people are sick in England, they "go to hospital." The article the is not used before "hospital."

EXAMPLE

The mail carrier just came. Here's **the** mail.
The new uniforms are red and gold.
Meet me at **the** library.

*The mail carrier is so friendly. What's our definite article in this last sentence? Is it **the?** It's true! **The** is most definitely the definite article.*

A and **an** are indefinite articles. They introduce a noun that could be any one thing within a group. For example, **a goldfish** can mean just any goldfish—not one certain goldfish.

How do you know whether to use **a** or **an?** Use **a** before a word beginning with a consonant or a consonant sound.

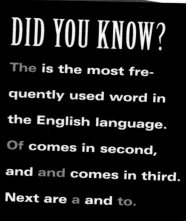

DID YOU KNOW?

The is the most frequently used word in the English language. **Of** comes in second, and **and** comes in third. Next are **a** and **to.**

How would you describe this picture? We could say that there's an elephant on the left and an elephant to the right. Or we could say, here are a couple of cute elephants. Indefinite articles help us to describe most everything we see.

Use **an** before a word beginning with a vowel or a vowel sound.

Suppose you went to the zoo. There you might see **a** kangaroo, **a** monkey, or **a** yak. Maybe you'd see **an** alligator, **an** elephant, **an** iguana, or **an** ostrich. You might even see **an** upside-down sloth!

CHAPTER SIX

NOUNS THAT ACT LIKE ADJECTIVES

Sometimes a noun acts like an adjective. It describes another noun.

Like many adjectives, it answers the question "which one?" or "what kind?" Here

are some examples:

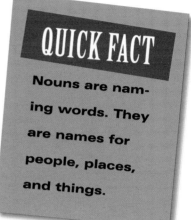

QUICK FACT

Nouns are naming words. They are names for people, places, and things.

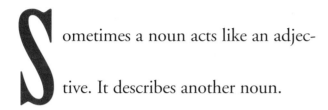

EXAMPLE

The family car is in the shop right now.
This is my favorite computer game.
Ten o'clock is story hour.
Someone left the porch light on.

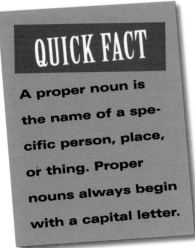

QUICK FACT

A proper noun is the name of a specific person, place, or thing. Proper nouns always begin with a capital letter.

Proper nouns can be changed into adjectives, too. Then they're called proper adjectives.

Like proper nouns, these adjectives begin with

a capital letter.

The class put on a **Hispanic** festival.

I love **Vietnamese** food.

Maya Angelou is an **African-American** poet.

Where's that **Harry Potter** book?

Let's watch the **New York** Giants play football!

*We love going to the Chicago street festival. In this last sentence, we are using the word **Chicago** as a proper adjective because it describes other nouns in the sentence.*

CHAPTER SEVEN

WHOSE IS IT?

There's another way nouns can act like adjectives. They can show who owns something. When nouns are used to show ownership, they become possessive adjectives. They're sometimes called possessive nouns. However, like all adjectives, they tell something about a noun.

DEFINITION

A possessive adjective shows ownership.

You can often spot a possessive adjective right away. It has an apostrophe ('). To turn most singular nouns into possessive adjectives, just add an apostrophe + *s*.

EXAMPLE

the song of the **bird** = the **bird's** song
the hideout of **Anna** = **Anna's** hideout
the orders of the **boss** = the **boss's** orders

If papa bird's little baby birds are hungry, what is our possessive adjective?
*It's **bird's**, because **bird's** indicates that the babies belong to papa bird.*

What about a plural noun? It already has an *-s* on the end. What

if you want to turn a plural noun into a possessive? In most cases, you

just add an apostrophe after the *-s*.

E X A M P L E

the den of the **lions** = the **lions'** den

the nests of the **birds** = the **birds'** nests

the house of the **Smiths** = the **Smiths'** house

A few plural nouns do not end with -*s*. In that case, you create the

possessive by adding apostrophe + *s*.

EXAMPLE

> **books for children = children's books**
> **a club for women = women's club**
> **clothes for men = men's clothes**

Sometimes you use a possessive word as a short way to

say something.

EXAMPLE

> **I'm going to the doctor's.**   (doctor's office)
> **I'm going to Jason's.**   (Jason's house)
> **I attend Saint John's.**   (Saint John's School)

What if something has more than one owner? Then only the last

owner gets the apostrophe + *s*.

EXAMPLE

> **Ben and Jerry's ice cream**
> **Mom and Dad's car**

CHAPTER EIGHT

PRONOUNS THAT ACT LIKE ADJECTIVES

Suppose everyone brought a frog to school. Then all the frogs were put in one big cage. How could you point out which frog is whose? You might use pronouns that act like adjectives.

EXAMPLE

That's my frog! That's her frog! That's your frog!

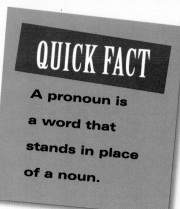

QUICK FACT

A pronoun is a word that stands in place of a noun.

All the red words above are pronouns showing who owns each frog. When pronouns are used to show ownership, they become possessive adjectives. They're sometimes called possessive pronouns. However, they're all acting like adjectives. Like all adjectives, they describe a noun.

*Is that frog your frog or his frog? **His** and **hers** and **theirs** and **yours** are all examples of possessive pronouns.*

*If the monkey turned its head and said, "ooh-ooh-ooh!" the word **its** would be a possessive adjective.*

WATCH OUT!

Watch out for the tricky possessives—**whose, its, your,** and **their.** Don't confuse them with contractions. Contractions combine two words and use an apostrophe ('). But possessive adjectives never get an apostrophe!

EXAMPLE

POSSESSIVE	**Whose** computer is this?
CONTRACTION	**Who's** (or, Who is) at the door?
POSSESSIVE	The monkey curled **its** tail up.
CONTRACTION	**It's** (or, It is) your turn.
POSSESSIVE	**Your** hamster is under the couch.
CONTRACTION	**You're** (or, You are) early today.
POSSESSIVE	**Their** window broke.
CONTRACTION	**They're** (or, They are) not home.

CHAPTER NINE

MORE PRONOUNS THAT ACT LIKE ADJECTIVES

Lots more pronouns can act like adjectives. Take the demonstrative pronouns—**this, that, these,** and **those.** You use them to demonstrate, or point things out. But if they come before a noun, they're acting like adjectives. Then they become demonstrative adjectives.

DEFINITION

A **demonstrative adjective** is used to show or point out something.

EXAMPLE

PRONOUN	ADJECTIVE
This is mine.	**This** frog is mine.
That is yours.	**That** turtle is yours.
These are dirty.	**These** sneakers are dirty.
Put **those** away!	Put **those** games away!

Now let's look at interrogative pronouns—**what, which,** and **whose.** They're used to ask questions. But when they describe a noun, they're acting like adjectives. Then they turn into interrogative adjectives.

*Whose old bike is that? It's impossible to know, but one thing we do know is that the word **whose** was used as an interrogative adjective. We know this because it was used to ask a question about a bike, which is a noun.*

DEFINITION

An interrogative adjective is used to ask a question.

EXAMPLE

PRONOUN	ADJECTIVE
What am I hearing?	**What** music am I hearing?
Which are yours?	**Which** shoes are yours?
Whose is this?	**Whose** bike is this?

CHAPTER TEN

FUN WITH NUMBERS AND OPPOSITES

You've been counting with adjectives since you were little.

Do you remember these?

*It's my eighth birthday, so why do I only have four candles on my cake? In this last sentence, **eighth** comes before birthday, which makes it a number adjective. **Four** comes before candles, so **four** is also a number adjective.*

EXAMPLE

I'm **three** years old!
My cake has **four** candles!
Look! I have **ten** fingers!

All the numbers above are adjectives. Each one tells something about a noun. They answer the question "how many?" Number adjectives can also tell what position something holds in a group.

This is the **twelfth** rainy day in a row.

My **first** lobster was too big to eat.

That's your **seventh** piece of cake!

Opposite adjectives can be lots of fun. People sometimes get into big arguments over them! In these examples, choose the opposite that's true for you. Then see if other kids answer the same way.

I like soup that's **hot/cold**.

My favorite music is **quiet/loud**.

Math is **easy/hard**.

Light/dark chocolate tastes the best.

I like clowns that look **happy/sad**.

Compact discs are **cheap/expensive**.

Turtles can be pretty **fast/slow**.

My best friend is **short/tall**.

How to Learn More

At the Library

Boynton, Sandra. *A Is for Angry.* New York: Workman Publishing, 1987.

Cleary, Brian P., and Jenya Prosmitsky (illustrator). *Hairy, Scary, Ordinary: What Is an Adjective?* Minneapolis: Carolrhoda, 2000.

Collins, S. Harold, and Kathy Kifer (illustrator). *Adjectives and Adverbs.* Eugene, Ore.: Garlic Press, 1990.

Gregorich, Barbara, and Usborne Books. *Adjectives and Adverbs.* Tulsa, Okla.: EDC Publications, 1999.

Maestro, Betsy, and Giulio Maestro (illustrator). *On the Go: A Book of Adjectives.* New York: Random House, 1988.

Walton, Rick, and Jimmy Holder (illustrator). *Pig Pigger Piggest.* Salt Lake City, Utah: Gibbs-Smith, 2003.

On the Web

Visit our home page for lots of links about grammar:
http://www.childsworld.com/links.html

NOTE TO PARENTS, TEACHERS AND LIBRARIANS: We routinely check our Web links to make sure they're safe, active sites—so encourage your readers to check them out!

Through the Mail or by Phone

To find a Grammar Hotline near you, contact:
THE GRAMMAR HOTLINE DIRECTORY
Tidewater Community College Writing Center
1700 College Crescent
Virginia Beach, VA 23453
Telephone: (757) 822-7170
http://www.tcc.edu/students/resources/writcent/GH/hotlino1/htm

To learn more about grammar, visit the Grammar Lady online or call her toll free hotline:
THE GRAMMAR LADY
Telephone: (800) 279-9708
www.grammarlady.com

Fun with Adjectives

Are you a poet? You will be when you choose rhyming adjectives

for these sentences.

1. Witches are _____, but Santa is _____.
   (merry, scary)

2. Clowns can be _____ unless they are _____.
   (chilly, silly)

3. When my oatmeal is _____, I get very _____.
   (lumpy, grumpy)

4. My puppy is _____, and his dog food is _____.
   (sticky, tricky)

5. I read when it's _____, and that's why I'm _____.
   (brainy, rainy)

Can you think of more rhyming adjectives and make poems out
of them?

See page 32 for the answers. Don't peek!

Index

-able, 5
-al, 5
apostrophe, 21, 22, 23, 25
articles, 15–16

comparative form, 9–10, 12, 13–14
consonants, 17, 18
contractions, 25

definite articles, 16
demonstrative adjectives, 26
demonstrative pronouns, 26
double comparisons, 12

-ed, 6
England, 16
-er, 9–10, 11
-est, 10–11

-ful, 5

indefinite articles, 17–18
-ing, 6
interrogative adjectives, 27
interrogative pronouns, 27

irregular comparative form, 11–12
-ive, 5

-less, 5
linking verbs, 7, 8

nouns, 4, 7, 16, 19–20, 22–23, 26
numbers, 28–29

opposite adjectives, 29
-ous, 5

plural nouns, 22–23
possessive adjectives, 21–22, 24–25
predicate adjectives, 7–8
pronouns, 4, 7, 24–27
proper nouns, 19–20

superlative form, 10–12

vowels, 18

-y, 5

Answers

Answers to Text Exercises

page 6

There are many possible answers.

Here are some suggestions:

good—excellent, pleasant, wonderful, super, great

old—ancient, antique, elderly

little—tiny, petite, small

great—extreme, fantastic, terrific, sensational

quiet—hushed, still, tranquil, muffled, silent

page 12

dark, darker, darkest

young, younger, youngest

new, newer, newest

strong, stronger, strongest

expensive, more expensive, most expensive

Answers to Fun with Adjectives

1. scary, merry
2. silly, chilly
3. lumpy, grumpy
4. tricky, sticky
5. rainy, brainy

About the Author

Ann Heinrichs was lucky. Every year from grade three through grade eight, she had a big, fat grammar textbook and a grammar workbook. She feels that this prepared her for life. She is now the author of more than 100 books for children and young adults. She has also enjoyed successful careers as a children's book editor and an advertising copywriter. Ann grew up in Fort Smith, Arkansas, and lives in Chicago, Illinois.